THE BETRAYAL

POEMS BY

MICHAEL D. HIGGINS

WITH DRAWINGS BY MICK MULCAHY

Grateful acknowledgement is made to the editors of the following
publications, in which some of these poems first appeared:
*The Salmon, Poetry Ireland Review, Z Magazine, Macalla,
Studies, The Sunday Tribune.*

Book design by Robert Armstrong
Typeset by Irish Typesetters, Galway
Printed by Colour Books, Dublin
Hardcover binding by Kenny's Fine Binding, Galway

ISBN O 948339 39 X Hardcover £10.95
ISBN O 948339 40 3 Softcover £6.95

Produced with the financial assistance of The Arts Council
(An Comhairle Ealaion), and Brendan Smith, Club Rapparee, Galway.

Salmon Publishing,
Auburn, Upper Fairhill, Galway, Ireland.

For Sabina, Alice-Mary, John Peter, Michael Edward and Daniel; and those in arts and politics in Ireland and abroad to whom I owe so much and who shared so much with me.

I would like to thank so many people who encouraged me to take my attempts at dealing with the broken rhetorics of politics, the academy, and private expressions, and turn them into the poems published here.

Brendan Kennelly was a source of much more than encouragement. He provided a sheltering place where I could make a fumbling rediscovery. Jessie Lendennie published *The Master* in 'The Salmon' and my silence was broken.

Margaret Shiel, Betty Dowling, Maureen Gordon and Josephine Donnelly-Nash bore the brunt of poems arriving like rain on a dry field of political correspondence.

Maureen Gordon was also a special source of sensitivity and criticism for the poems as they emerged. Ronan Sheehan was a special source of encouragement and assistance.

Seamus Hosey was my introduction to reading the poems publicly.

My gratitude also to Robert Armstrong and Siobhan Hutson, and special thanks to Mick Mulcahy who is much more than a friend, and who has become a partner in Art.

Contents

The Betrayal

A Poem for My Father

This man is seriously ill,
The doctor had said a week before,
Calling for a wheelchair.
It was
After they rang me
To come down
And persuade you
To go in
Condemned to remember your eyes
As they met mine in that moment
Before they wheeled you away.
It was one of my final tasks
To persuade you to go in,
A Judas chosen not by Apostles
But by others more broken;
And I was, in part,
Relieved when they wheeled you from me,
Down that corridor, confused,
Without a backward glance
And when I had done it,
I cried, out on the road,
Hitching a lift to Galway and away
From the trouble of your
Cantankerous old age
And rage too,
At all that had in recent years
Befallen you.

All week I waited to visit you
But when I called, you had been moved

To where those dying too slowly
Were sent,
A poorhouse, no longer known by that
    name,
But in the liberated era of Lemass,
Given a saint's name, 'St. Joseph's'.
Was he Christ's father,
Patron saint of the Worker,
The mad choice of some pietistic politician?
You never cared.

Nor did you speak too much.
You had broken an attendant's glasses,
The holy nurse told me,
When you were admitted.
Your father is a very difficult man,
As you must know. And Social Welfare is
    slow
And if you would pay for the glasses,
I would appreciate it.
It was 1964, just after optical benefit
Was rejected by De Valera for poorer classes
In his Republic, who could not afford,
As he did
to travel to Zurich
For their regular tests and their
Rimless glasses.

It was decades earlier
You had brought me to see him

Pass through Newmarket-on-Fergus
As the brass and reed band struck up,
Cheeks red and distended to the point
Where a child's wonder was as to whether
They would burst as they blew
Their trombones.
The Sacred Heart Procession and De Valera,
You told me, were the only occasions
When their instruments were taken
From the rusting, galvanised shed
Where they stored them in anticipation
Of the requirements of Church and State.

Long before that, you had slept,
In ditches and dug-outs,
Prayed in terror at ambushes
With others who later debated
Whether De Valera was lucky or brilliant
In getting the British to remember
That he was an American.
And that debate had not lasted long
In concentration camps in Newbridge
And the Curragh, where mattresses were
    burned,
As the gombeens decided that the new State
Was a good thing,
Even for business.

In the dining-room of St. Joseph's
The potatoes were left in the middle of the
    table
In a dish, towards which

You and many other Republicans
Stretched feeble hands that shook.
Your eyes were bent as you peeled
With the long thumb-nail I had often
    watched
Scrape a pattern on the leather you had
    toughened for our shoes,
Your eyes when you looked at me
Were a thousand miles away,
Now totally broken,
Unlike those times even
Of rejection, when you went at sixty
For jobs you never got,
Too frail to load vans, or manage
The demands of selling.
And I remember
When you came back to me,
Your regular companion of such occasions,
And said, They think that I'm too old
For the job. I said I was fifty-eight
But they knew that I was past sixty.

A body ready for transportation,
Fit only for a coffin, that made you
Too awkward
For death at home.
The shame of a coffin exit
Through a window sent you here,
Where my mother told me you asked
Only for her to place her cool hand
Under your neck.
And I was there when they asked
Would they give you a Republican funeral,

In that month when you died,
Between the end of the First Programme for
     Economic Expansion
And the Second.

I look at your photo now,
Taken in the beginning of bad days,
With your surviving mates
In Limerick.
Your face haunts me as do these memories;
And all these things have been scraped
In my heart,
And I can never hope to forget
What was, after all,
A betrayal.

Relatives Assisting

A room in the house
And a seat in the car to Mass,
That was the promise made in wills
To look after those
Who did not travel,
But chose instead
To ride High Nelly bicycles to Church
On Sundays, where they knelt
In the women's aisle, and listened
To visiting missioners thunder about
The sins of the flesh, and how
Queen Elizabeth had died,
Rolled in a ball in agony, screaming
For the True Church. It was too late,
Of course, and it was a good feeling
For even a little while to be pure.
The Child of Mary medal was a consolation
And would travel with them
To the grave. And in the room guaranteed
You could prepare your black
And save shillings from sales of eggs and
    butter
For porter at your wake.
'Relatives Assisting',
They called you on the forms.
You had no acres, no lovers, no children,
But you had
What was more important
A room in the house
And a seat in the car to Mass,
And in the meantime,
Your High Nelly bicycle
And your prayers.

The Master

There once was an old Master who was
Very cold
Each morning outside his school
He'd line them up,
Shine your shoes children
Be erect.
Shine your shoes or you will
Gather faggots from ditches
For the School, for the Parish, for
Jesus and the Civil Service
Shine your shoes.

Inside the school awaiting the Inspector
He'd stand little girls on desks
And lash their calves
Until the weals showed
And the tears came,
Know your verbs or you're going
Nowhere, he'd shout
You'll be gathering faggots from
Ditches
For the School, for the Parish, for
Jesus and the Civil Service,
Learn your verbs.

At evening going home
The villagers would avoid his gaze
Catching their eye the Master might
Not even nod.
They always froze
For he was a cold man.

It was rumoured that even rabbits
Caught in his gaze
Would sit
As caught in a light
And wait to die.

At four his wife would say
The Master's home
Children finish your tea
Blessing himself he would eat
For he was a religious man
But he would not speak.
His wife
Bearer of their children
Would occasionally whisper
The Master's thinking.

In his room he would sink to his
Knees and pray
Oh Jesus I've done all this for you
I've brought order
I've brought discipline
For the School, for the Parish and
For you Jesus
And I've sent them to the Civil Service
Send me a sign.

And thus it was that one evening
In a blue haze
To his room a lady came.

My Son asked me to come, she said
For He was afraid of you Himself
And He told me to tell you
For Mothers must always bring
Messages
That He said it all on the Mount,
Love everybody
But particularly,
Love yourself.

The Master jumped from his knees
And tearing off his clothes
Laughed and ran from the room
I've had a sign, he told his wife
I've had a vision.

Running into the street the
Villagers heard the Master's
Cries
I've had a sign
I've had a vision.

He ran to the edge of a wood
Where they found him
Embracing a tree.

At first they were timid
For they were, after all, his pupils
At one time or another
And the braver threw a blanket over him.

Saying with a soothing repetition,
Yes, Master, of course Master,

You've had a sign
You've had a vision.

And they brought him to hospital
Where all he would say was
I've had a sign
I've had a vision.

At first the villagers simply said
To each other, in pubs
Imagine the Master, of all people,
And then much later, in shops,
It could happen to any of us.

They visited him in hospital
And they brought him books
Which he never read
Saying simply
With a smile that shocked them
I've had a sign
I've had a vision.

And after a while the villagers were
Happy to hear the news from the hospital.
They've allowed him to arrange the flowers
    on the altar
Isn't that nice, some said.
And in the hospital the Matron watched
    with pleasure
As the Master the flowers in perfect taste
    arranged
But shook her head as she heard him say
I've had a sign
I've had a vision.

And it was a Sunday ritual
That his wife and children would come
And he would smile at them and say,
I'll tell you a secret,
Love everybody, but particularly
Love yourself
That was my vision.
And it was on such an occasion
That his son burst out,
Father, fuck your vision
Stop this nonsense
And they'll let you out.

But the Master looked at him and wept
And then he smiled and said,
Do not ask me to go back
Do not hurt yourself,
No, my son
Love everybody
But particularly love yourself
That was my vision.
His son wept and shook his young head
And in the village they concluded
That the Master was indeed mad.

Jesus Appears in Dublin in 1990 at the Port & Docks Board Site

It created a sensation.
The T.V. Cameras were there.
Everybody was weeping
When Jesus appeared in Dublin
At the Port and Docks Board Site
In 1990.
The ageing Prime Minister tried to be
   photographed with him
But Jesus was having none of it.

I've come myself, he said,
For I'm tired of sending my mother
And I wanted to say how pleased I am
That you've stopped all that nonsense
They press-released from me on the Mount.
The embargo was scarcely over
When I knew it was all a dreadful mistake.
The truth is I'm European now like you.

Tough measures are necessary in these
   difficult times,
As you busy men know.
Let the children be without books.
Words and books are dangerous things.
Let the aged die in silence.
They talk too much.

And get rid of all that stuff of ripening
   youth.
Or the roots of the tree will give way
Under the rot of their fallen expectations.

The sick are not really sick.
We all know that in our hearts.
You work, you live, you tell them,
And you're right.
Those old solidarities are evil,
It is the I that counts.

And all that business about the
   money-lenders
In the Temple,
The truth is I never meant it.
They were of your kind,
Far too smart,
Far too quick
For me.

I confess.
I confess.
Try to forgive me.
And even my mother knows I've wronged
   you.

And she will come again to you all
And I'll try to be a European.
The tears flowed down his white Caucasian
   face.
The crowd threw themselves on the ground,
Littered with Coca-Cola tins,
And looked up at the sky and said,
Oh God,
Thank you for sending your son
And preparing us for 1992.

Our Beautiful Yute

From the skull it came
One morning,
My poem.

For years I'd brought it on the train
And sometimes,
If I'd been drinking
Perhaps,
I'd let it out.

And thus it was
I brought it to the Members' Bar of the Dáil.
Where a friend said
He'd like to see it in a book
But I had brought it round with me for
    years
And kept it mostly in my skull.
I did not want it trapped in print
And thus it was
I let it out again
To play one evening
With a gaggle of T.D.s

They were playing a game called
Our Beautiful Yute,
Invented in a party with a "th" defect.
The contest was to see
Who had the most lacrimose glands.
They'd weep for unemployment.
They'd weep for emigration.
They'd weep for the really poor,
But not for deserted wives.

In the game of the lacrimose glands
The prize was reserved for the one
Who shed the largest tears
For Our Beautiful Yute.

They stopped their game for a little while
And listened coldly to the intruder,
My poem.

He's very sad, one said.
He's very bitter, said another.
I don't recognise him, said most.
He doesn't even live in a book,
Said a wise one.
He won't even help us weep.
Let's go back to our game of the lacrimose
    glands, Playing
Our Beautiful Yute.

I put him back in my skull
And said,
One day, and not in drink,
I'll release you, poem.
I will not lock you in a book
Where they might dissect you
Or leave you uncared,
Where they might eject you
From any game,
Even the game of the lacrimose glands
Called
Our Beautiful Yute.

And in the meantime, we'll travel,
You and I,
Even if it is only in my skull
You will travel.
We'll go together to strange places
Where I'll let you out
And I promise you
It will never be where you are told
That you have some defect
That disqualifies you
From the game of the lacrimose glands
Called
Our Beautiful Yute.

And in the meantime,
My poem,
My love,
You must remain,
However uncomfortable for us both,
In my skull.

Requiem for a Parish Priest

He stands at the window
The old Parish Priest with rheumy eyes
His eyes catch the graveyard stones
As he holds his glass of sherry.
Later after tea and scrambled eggs
It will be port or brandy.

The status anamarum lies finished
On the mahogany table
His hand trembles
As he thinks of God and souls
How often had he spoken of such things
And on occasion lately
But much more rarely
Of Jesus.

The book of homilies lies open
Make it relevant, it said,
Use images.
Life is like knitting a jumper
If you drop a stitch
Go back,
Unravel and pick it up again.
Too trite.

And anyway he was too old for all this stuff
Of Jesus and knitting
He sinks into the black leather chair
His sister bought
When he got his first Parish
The smell of leather still mingled
With tobacco and sherry.

Leaving Maynooth so long ago
He would have mocked
Such a throne
Idealistic then
When things were simple
Twas easily known
When souls were won and lost
When shepherds called the shots
And good sheep knew their place.

But was it not these halcyon days
Of simple truth that ruined his life
His housekeeper was the first to notice his
    doubt
Afraid to speak she hid the bottles
Bringing them away,
Not putting them in the bin,
For discretion's sake
And before that first visit to St Pat's
He foxed her with whiskey in hot water
    bottles
It was the soul that needed warmth
Not his body
He'd told himself.

He'd lasted through a lot
For days when he shared glasses of stout
    with reverential farmers.
Who later mocked him when his words
    were slurred.

Their children wide-eyed eating marietta
   biscuits
Wondered why the priest was strange
Even if it was in the snug he sang
Or wandered through sections of Canon
   Sheehan.

Always on the morning after
He would tremble as he thought of lifting
   the Host
Or sweating he struggled through the
   Communion
His bishop advised him at first to rest
And later to pull himself together
As he gave him a remote parish.

He took to writing verse
The soul is not a garden
But a parlour overcrowded
With bric a brac, he'd written.
It didn't work as his mind wandered
Over memories of lost times
Forgotten friends
And a life lost
On truths too carelessly embraced.

He stayed alone while he was sober
Some said of course
When they discussed such things in the
   parish

As they did in hushed tones
That he was holy
That he was an ascetic
The doctor's wife used that word
For she was educated.
The older women said
That he was holy
That he could cure baldness in children
Ringworm and warts
The rumour was general.

The tears fill the eyes grown small
In a red area of facial flesh.
He turns away and a smile breaks
That is what they all missed
Was Christ's face not swollen in the garden
Had he not been reduced
To being a sorcerer.
And did they not know then in their hearts
Who suffered alone.
He would have his scrambled eggs
And after that a port
Or perhaps a brandy
And wait for them to call
About baldness in children
Ringworm and warts
And maybe
In healing them all
He'd heal himself.

Life Skills Course for Joyriders

It was after a few silent moments of quiet
   reflection,
After which he said he'd like to share a few
   thoughts with us,
And he'd be asking us later, he assured us,
As to whether we were sure
We were relating to each other,
That the gorgeous young priest
Began to talk of sex.

Men are like a powerful B.M.W., he said.
He knew we never stole a banger.
He was of the new breed
Of tuned in,
Switched on,
Wired up
Young priests
And he confided in us
That his bishop felt
He could relate to the likes of us.

A man is like a B.M.W., he said,
For when you've switched on the engine
You don't know the power
You've got under your foot.

A woman, on the other hand,
Is like a lamp-post.
They need only blink
And you'll go crashing in.
She doesn't know it
But she attracts that B.M.W.

Am I relating to you, he asked?
We told him that he was.

Now have a buzz session among yourselves,
He said,
While we all have coffee and chocolate
   biscuits,
And after our break
We'll have a role-playing session,
Which was not what we thought.
Some of you,
He continued,
Can be B.M.W.'s
And others can be lamp-posts.

And as for me,
He laughed,
Just think of me as the mechanic
Or the man in the pits
You might have seen on television on
   Saturdays.
But nobody wanted to be a lamp-post
And everybody a B.M.W.

Now isn't that interesting?
He said.
You all want to be B.M.W.'s.
You're wanting to be switched on,
To feel the power under your feet.
But have you allowed for the lamp-posts?
There will always be that type of girl.

I know a great deal about these things.
In our job we have to know
For your sake
Things you may not know.
They will be anxious to switch you on,
To make you pound on your accelerator
And send you crashing
To God's scrapyard in the skies.
Those lamp-posts are dangerous,
They will not only switch you on
But send you out of control.
Even leave you dead,
He blessed himself,
Just fit for scrap.

At lunch we stole the gorgeous young
    priest's car
And drove at eighty towards the Phoenix
    Park.
We waved at all the lamp-posts.
They never winked
Or even blinked
In our direction.

When we returned
He told us he was disappointed,
That obviously we could not relate
To what he had to say,
That we had not reflected
On what he was sharing with us.
So we told him all we knew

About sex,
And B.M.W.'s
And lamp-posts.

He wept
And thanked us
And promised us that
He'd never come again
To life-skills class
And talk about his car.
He'd come on a bicycle
Or on the Dart.
And we all laughed
'Cos, as the ould wans said,
It was all so funny.
After all
None of us could remember
How long it had been,
Since we'd stolen a bicycle
And we'd never got as far
As stealing a train.
And the Dart had never crashed
Into a lamp-post,
Even one that blinked.

Nocturne 1

How can I face you, Night
Alone,
Or shall I share my terror,
Exchanging obligation for fear?

For some, no doubt,
You bring relief,
Tired bones
Stretched in sleep.

But I dread your shadows
Ushering in thoughts
I cannot forget
Which demand an answer
To that ultimate question;

And when morning breaks,
Some greet it with a smile,
Lovely day today;
And I can only sigh.

Toil, toil, toil,
Talk, talk, talk,
And, even with a drink,
Pretence at intellectual conversation.

But, then you come,
Night,
With your terror,
Your reminder.
Why do you not claim your victory now?

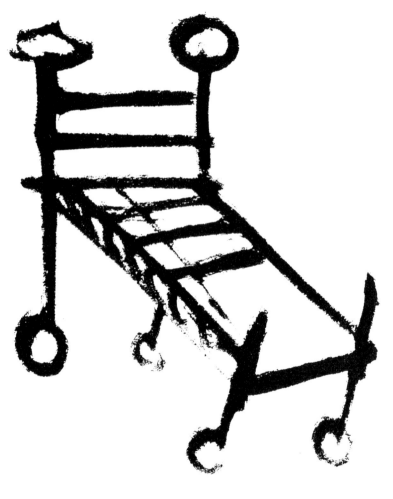

The Hole in the Heart Lover

The child that was not satisfied
With love
Becomes the man
That is some other woman's child Lover,
That cannot be cured
Of this hole in the heart
By cuddles, fondles or the warmest
   embraces.

And if this lover can be cured
By some cosmic surgery
It is perhaps by tears.
But if that works
Why is the world not full of tears?

And maybe that is why
The Greeks believed
The world was filled with water.
Was that water the tears of gods,
Made divine
And who thereby could not love?

How fortunate those
Children of love
Who with energy
Can freely embrace
And love
Beneath
Perhaps the envious gaze of the gods.

And if this remedy,
This cosmic surgery of tears
Fails,
There is but the ether
Of drink or children.

Then the man child lover
Is right to weep
And wonder
If the gaze
He gives his children is sufficient
To save them
From the genetic terror
Of their man child father's gift
Of being a hole in the heart lover.

The Prison

At the opening of Pentonville
The industrialists came.
Anxious to observe
The newly invented control
Of the body, time and space.
Their factories posed the same problems.
It was Truly marvellous,
As the Prince Consort said.
At one signal,
All doors could be unlocked.
From one point in space
All movements observed.
Taking off their silk hats,
They cheered
And pounded their canes
In celebration of this miracle
Of the new technology of order,
Time and space conquered.
They allowed themselves a moment
For kindly thoughts of Bentham,
His dream realised,
All movement, time and space
Made useful.

Time had been broken and counted
So long before in monastery cells,
Where it had been made necessary
To establish an accurate quantification
Of sin
And the penitential exorcisms necessary

First, of the body,
Later, of the mind
And, so much later, the soul,
The state of which excited
The interest of reformers,
Like Howard, who wrote
That he cried out in anguish
At the blackness of his own soul
When he dared envisage
The Countenance of the Lord,
Whose Name was so often invoked
In these places.

In Pentonville, the masked faces
In the numbered pew,
Boxed apart,
Could only stare at the pulpit
From which the preacher asked them
For repentance,
Not for murders or some great injury
But theft of two and six
By a fifty year old woman,
Or two rabbits
By a twelve year old boy.
Around their necks
They carry numbers and photos
For the records show
That prisons were built much more
For the poor
Than the wicked.

Should they work
Or read the Bible?
The debate raged
On both sides of the Atlantic.
In solitary
Some saved their souls.
Many more went mad,
As Tocqueville found.
And workers were scarce
For the roads, the fields, the mines, the
    swamps.

In England the crowd got drunk, waiting
For the condemned man to piss himself
On the scaffold.
It was moved inside
The prison walls
Where a bell rang out
When life had gone
And quicklime waited.
And it was all revenge.

The body, time and space made tame,
The mind was next.
They called it deviance now.
New experts knew what was a mind
Gone mad.
For years, waiting for death,
They lingered,
Unsafe for human-kind,
In harness and padded cells.
Or, if they were good,
Involved with acts of piety

In front of altars,
Or on their knees in flower beds.

Law and order, was the cry.
You need it, and control,
When the pills don't work,
For life was prison now
And had dissolved
To reach all pain
In schools and hospitals,
Where choice was dangerous
And answers were available
To all but those too troublesome
To listen to those who knew.
The man gone mad from poteen can't
    remember
When he did it,
Burned his house
When his love died,
And was brought by neighbours
To the mental hospital.

When morning breaks in Mountjoy Gaol,
Two dozen pots are emptied in a tank
Where men will later wash,
And pay the price demanded
In lost privacy.
In Loughan House, young jackeens rarely
    gaze in wonder
At the beauty of a West of Ireland dawn.
They think of flats, of fags and cars
In cities that were their homes.

And in the papers, the cry is out.
In Leinster House it is the same.
We need more prisons for our youth.
We need them for our safety.
After all, our wives,
Our children, even our cars
Are not safe
From the thugs, the savages
And those who unlike us
Have never learned
To know their place.

A Race Night Reflection in the University City of Galway, 1970

Evening breaks over the fast greening
Copper dome of Galway's Cathedral.
In Peter Michael's, mirth is forsaken for
  grief,
However brief,
As funeral time approaches.
Bury the dead properly.
The widow arranges to weep.
In another room a drunken father
Welcomes an accidental son,
Born into a world he'll never understand.
Students pass carrying books and jotters,
Notes half-carelessly taken from
The yellowed lecture notes
Of professors who have long lost interest.
The funeral emerges.
Draw the blinds.
Respect the dead.
Popular man that.
Fair amount of cars,
From Castlegar they say.

Down town, the lawyers
With long legal faces
Fresh from the High Court in circuit,
Are trying to decide whether to leave the
  Tavern
To travel for oysters in Clarinbridge
Or to settle for the Claddagh Grill.
Exchanging stories loudly, they command
  respect,

As they should, people of substance.
Wearers of wigs by morning,
Their Adam's Apples scarcely give as the
  afternoon claret
Salves their memories of clients.

We must remember it is Race Week
When all Galway comes alive,
Dead expectations of sex,
Or even love, resurface.
Thin-lipped Julia, sipping brandy in a
  corner,
From a glass that intimidates,
Casts eyes half furtively
At a loud mouthed farmer, strayed in,
Whom, more likely, she should despise.
Thinking carefully, she turns her body,
No longer beautiful but protected,
In the direction of those more likely
  respectable,
And sighs.

In the Cellar Bar
You who called yourself "Mate",
Are bumming the price of pints
From sleeveens half your worth,
Balancing yourself to ask,
In your own well-turned phrase,
How're you fixed for the rough touch?
Yours the lesser request,

Paid for with a wit that was not acquired
At Chamber of Commerce meetings
But in the flux of life itself.
You will be missed by those who loved or
    cared,
Not by the huxters
For whom the till rings loud.

Estate agents, insurance brokers and
    bankers,
This is your week.
Above all others, you talk indiscreetly
Of looking after your figures
And playing squash,
Adequate replacement for intellect.
But let us not be bitter.
Are your wives not beautiful,
At a price?
They concentrate
On not letting you down in public
As they spray sherry
From glasses held in inexperienced hands,
Forgetting that one occasion
When ribs were broken in their rush
Towards a visiting Irish-American President
At a garden party in Aras an Uachtarain.

In Riley's Pub
A few older men with red faces,
Indicating the evening of a life
Devoted to porter and patriotism,

Look uncomfortably at their successors
In green second-hand jackets,
Who talk of Republicanism by day
And at night, being consistent,
Whet their thirst
And, not forgetting principle,
Sing "Joe Hill"
For benefit of passion and profit.

In the Great Southern Hotel,
A man regarded as mad
For interrupting a Bishop in his Cathedral,
Saying he'd heard it all before
Seized by Knights of Columbanus in Christ's
    House,
And cured by E.C.T. in Ballinasloe,
Tells American tourists he wants them
To join with him
In saying the Rosary in the foyer
For the boys in Vietnam.
Chaos reigns among the bags
As porters struggle
To defeat the prayers.
He is told that he is barred,
The hotel made safe for winners at the
    Races,
Where once the sleeveens shouted
When Máirtin Mór McDonagh's horse came
    home
In the Galway Plate in 1934.
Lead him in yourself, Mr Máirtin,

They to whom Máirtin Mór gave a free
  coffin
For a lifetime in his service,
Owning them in life
Boxing them in death.
Tonight his spirit will no doubt rejoice
With those who've come for the Galway
  Races.

Walking past your great stone Cathedral,
I cannot but think of you, cross Michael of
  Galway,
Pompous heir of the Apostles.
You saved us your presence this night,
Alone at home on the night of the Galway
  Races.
More charitable perhaps
Than they say
You stayed at home,
Musing perhaps over the irrelevancies
You would inflict on Sunday;
Lonely, friend of none save those
Too tired or too cowed to question
A metaphysics long out-dated,
You pour a glass of wine or port
And remember better days
When Russell was proved in error
To the applause of reverend fathers, sisters,
Ladies and gentlemen,
Two hundred nuns

And a hundred apprentice Franciscans,
On St Thomas Aquinas's Day
In the Aula Maxima of U.C.G.
Brilliant but wrong, Cathal Daly said
To tumultuous applause.
But you outdid Cathal in your day
In Natural Law,
Arguing for the distinction
Between false teeth and condoms.

And now I must return
To the irrelevancy of my own earned
  madness,
Look fearfully at students, disinterested,
Wanting their introduction to commerce,
Blessed with unconcern,
Anxious to serve, escape,
Who knows, grow rich.

I have exhausted my concession
And it is time to go and take my place
Where the mad and foolish lodge.
And after all, the morning will break on a
  new day
After the Galway Races.

Stargazer

For Mary Coyne

She stands,
Supported by her stick,
In front of the gilt mirror
Her husband bought
In a mad moment,
After selling the calves in Claremorris,
In the first year of their marriage.

Neck stretched back,
She drops the lotion
In her one good eye.
The tears come
And she remembers,
In her solitary kitchen,
Times when she stretched her neck back
To show the stars to her seven children.

Uranus, Mars, Venus and the Milky Way
In the canopy over Claremorris.
She had traced them all
With her bright bride's eyes.

The tears come from her one good eye
For her scattered children
And her children's children,
Seed of her seed.
The range is cold that once was warm.
On it she rests her hand,
And remembers
Times when, pressing her forehead

Against the warm udder of a cow,
Reluctant milk-giver,
She told them stories from Dickens,
Of Ham and Twist:
And always they would say,
But tonight, will you show us the stars.

She stretches back again
To drop the lotion in her one good eye.
Alone, she steadies herself
And cranes her neck.
The darkness comes as the drops fall
On her one good eye.
And through the mist of tears,
She sees the empty kitchen.

There is nobody to ask now for the stars.
There is only silence
And the memories of a world emptied of
    people,
Of feeling.
She straightens in front of the gilt mirror
And wipes the tears from her face,
Lined with a thousand stories.
Sleep was but a dark night,
And death a journey to the stars.

Mother of mothers,
Stargazer,
Dust of dust,

Tonight, you say,
You do not need your one good eye
To read the signs of sky by night.
To read alone was all you asked,
Be told of distant things,

Go out tonight
Stargazer
And plot your journey home.

The Age of Granola

It was in the age of Granola
When you had long flowing hair
And people turned when we laughed
For they deeply coveted the reason
That we with so little
Were free

It was in the age of Granola
That our bodies were supple and thin
And our friends kept asking how you did it,
You had such beautiful skin.
But at night you told them of Miso,
On buses they wondered
When you went all serious about Zen.

It was in the age of Granola
When you wore a massive black hat,
That I burned the rubbish of guilt
And it really didn't take much effort
For love to find its way in.

And that's why we never really saw it,
The wave that was coming our way.

In Moscow they're queuing for McDonalds,
In Tokyo Bud is the choice
And freedom brings pills to the South.
And we never saw that it was coming,
The whole world was going to be free.

When the Muse Visits

for Brendan Kennelly

Poet, do not complain when the Muse visits.
Welcome her in your warm abrazo.*
Or are you too tired for her subversive
    touch?
A viejo* who puts sleep before the touch of
    flesh?

If she is not made welcome,
She will not leave, but sigh,
And stay with you for a while.
As all love dies,
It will not be sudden.
It will simply wither.

Poet, hold the Muse in your embrace.
Exhaust yourself and celebrate.
Fashion into words
That which most may feel
But never utter.

What you are allowed
In the foreplay of the soul, is sacred.
You have been chosen, poet,
Hold the Muse con respeto*
In your embrace.

*   *abrazo* embrace
*   *viejo* old man
*   *con respeto* with respect

Nocturne 2

Listening to your laboured breathing
My daughter
I pray,
Yes, I do,
That your life will be unlike mine:
That you be loved,
Be free
From guilt
And all anxiety:
That you draw nothing from my genes,
Of the cursed blackness
I brought upon myself
By efforts to escape.

I was no condor
Meant to soar above the Andes,
Fed upon the blood
Of a mad bull.

We are not condors.
We do not fly.
We drink
For strength to kill
All love that surrounds us.
Those captured early,
Roped,
Chained.
Our scraggy necks
Reveal it all.

Turn over and wait, poet,
For the earth
Food for worms,
Themselves made for death
Perhaps
Dramatically
At the hands of some gravedigger's spade.

Go on,
I'll go on.
Rob Beckett of a few words.
And was Walt Whitman right
That it was enough
At evening
To stretch a warm hand
Along the warm back
Of anyone that loved,
Temporarily
Taken for excitement.

What is this poetry
But the last rattle of the bag
The four or five stabbings
Of the organ
They had the arrogance
To call the Flesh,
The name chosen
By God's Son amongst Catholics.
Or is it some dragged out
Frantic excitation

From an old foreskin of knowledge
Tranquiliser of night
Or a demented moment,
A masturbation of bad memories,
Guilt or lost opportunities
Which in an arrogant moment
They call
The dark night of the soul?

Comhluadar

Is cuimhin liom go maith,
Bailithe ar bhruach na h-uaighe,
Daoine a ceapadh 'bheith mór
An lá sin, umhal,
Is faoin bhfothaín leo na boicht.
Comhluadar faoi bhrón.

Is an t-am go léir
Glór na h-ithreach ag tuitim,
Cré ar adhmadh,
Tusa imithe,
Buartha briste ag an saol.
Bagairt na ceiste orm—
Cén fáth?
Cromthai briste,
Imithe faoin bhfód,
Uaigh lán,
Comhluadar ag scaipeadh.
Ach an cheist fágtha liomsa—
Cén fáth?
Comhluadar féin—Cé hiad?
Gan bhaint acu lenár fhulaing tú
Gan freastal ar an gceist—
Cén fáth?
B'fhéidhir gur gá ceol na cré
Chun comhluadar a bhailiú seal.

Ach tá tú imíthe
Comhluadar scaipthe,
Is an cheist gan freagra.
Nach trua
Go mbeidh a leithéid ann arís.

Song of the Ivy

The ivy's leaves are bright and green.
Don't bring it home,
Our mother said,
There's bad luck in that ivy.

I plucked its branch and laughed
And ran
And said it was like holly
Whose berries fed the birds
And made our Christmas folly.

But later now her voice comes back,
Our bodies old,
Our spirits weak,
No blossoms now,
No fragrant Spring.

The ivy's leaves are bright and green.
Don't bring it home,
Our mother said,
There's bad luck in that ivy.

When we were young my leaves
Were bright,
I twined around your bark.
I hid your silver from the sun
And both of us grew tall.
You pushed your limbs past my embrace
And blossomed for the Spring.

The ivy's leaves are bright and green.
Don't bring it home,
Our mother said,
There's bad luck in that ivy.

I fed on your young sap and grew
And slowly you grew tired;
And yet you could not leave.
I wrapped your broken wood with green
And covered you from light.

The ivy's leaves are bright and green.
Don't bring it home,
Our mother said,
There's bad luck in that ivy.

The ivy cannot love the tree,
Its green can only kill,
And yet we live together still
For is it love that trees must die
While locked in ivy's twines?

The ivy's leaves are bright and green.
Don't bring it home,
Our mother said,
There's bad luck in that ivy.

Was I the ivy to your life,
Did I ensnare your beauty,
Did I demand your juice and love

Until I killed your blossoms?
Oh, cut my roots, I often prayed,
Let my own captive live.

The ivy's leaves are bright and green.
Don't bring it home,
Our mother said,
There's bad luck in that ivy.

Oh, tear me from her bark, I prayed,
That she might see the sun,
Might laugh and sprout
And shout with life
And hear the singing bird.

The ivy's leaves are bright and green.
Don't bring it home,
Our mother said,
There's bad luck in that ivy.

Don't tear him from my bark, she said,
Don't leave me bare and weak,
For I am young no longer
And cannot face the light.
Oh, let me die in his embrace
For I have kissed the ivy.

The ivy's leaves are bright and green.
Don't bring it home,
Our mother said,
There's bad luck in that ivy.

For what is luck
And what is light
And did we not caress?
I fed his deadly cold green leaves
And felt his strangling grip.
If I were free I might have lived
But I had kissed the ivy.

The ivy's leaves are bright and green.
Don't bring it home,
Our mother said,
There's bad luck in that ivy.

Message for an Elder Statesman who defined Himself once as a Liberal rather than a Socialist

I remember it well those days,
Late in 1969,
When, behind badly scrawled banners,
We marched together.
And you joined us, marching more slowly;
And we,
Respecting your age, slowed our tread.
But now,
Our demands forgotten,
Be careful, elder statesman,
How deeply
You trample our banners
Into the gutter.

The Man Who Never Had A Visitor

They all knew about him
But nobody ever spoke
To the man who never had a visitor
In St Teresa's Ward
He had come so long ago
Nobody could remember.

It was the neighbours who brought him in
They heard,
On a strange night,
Of a high tide.

He spoke occasionally to the bushes
Or arranging the flowers in vases
He would be heard to whisper
But I know, I know
Why I did it.

In the village the story was well known
Of the man who burned his wife's house
Together they'd lived for thirty years
Without benefit of chick nor child
But he would look at her
In a slow way that they both knew
Was love in a time when softness was not
    allowed.
And the day he found her
Stretched in front of the fire
The tongs grasped in her hand
He screamed and ran from the house.

It was poitín that made the funeral pass
The neighbours shovelled out the clay
From his mother's grave
And one dead lover met another
And it was poitín too that did it,
They said.

When weeping in the corner of the bar
He could take it no more
And never returned home.

The priest, a young man, came
And brought him home
Pull yourself together Colie, he said
Life must go on

But all he could see was the dresser
And the two plates where she left them
And the two mugs
And the two chairs

There was two of everything
There will be one of nothing,
He screamed
And ran outside
The Man whose lover had died
And coming back
He brought a can
Asking the priest to come outside,
He cast the petrol at the gable thatch

And as his house burned he fell to his knees
And tears came
And he shook and screamed
They said it was the poitín
But all he said was
I will not let it be.
There was two of everything
There will be one of nothing.

And the neighbours saw the flames
Of the house of the man
Whose lover was gone.
My God, they said, he must be mad
To burn his cosy little house.
And they brought him here
On a strange night,
Of a high tide. And
They all knew about him
But nobody ever spoke
To the man who never had a visitor
In St. Teresa's ward.
He had come so long ago
Nobody could remember.

And in the village they didn't speak
Of the terrible things
That happened on a strange night
Of a high tide
When a man went mad
And burned his house

Screaming only
There was two of everything
There will be one of nothing.
There were many things better
Left unsaid
And some poor people best
Forgotten.

The Circle

It's when the circle closes,
No courage left for encounters
Offering new experiences,
Relationships.
That's when it is,
The closed circle
Offers its security
Of those familiar and safe.
Is it age
Or the death of courage?
For, after all,
Russell began so late a new relationship
With dead ideas.

Outside the circle it's noisy,
Some say, dangerous.
You'd need to know what you're doing,
Rely on advice of taxi-drivers,
Hotel staff and all those
Energised by a tip.
In your youth you'd lived
The fantasy,
Were open to all
The experience of life.
I won't die wondering,
You'd quoted the old waitress
Divorcee
Who swung her ample bottom at you
When, as a student
You thought it was all laid out before you.

Now it's your turn
To rely on the predictable
Reproduction of safe environments,
Fantasies abandoned,
You shuffle
With what you had of experience,
Ransacking,
Comparing against the fantasy,
You need your circle now.

It is not age alone.
It is not the void of courage spent.
It is maybe some ancient fear,
Against which there is no defence,
Not even the cold blade of reason,
A hollow gift itself when the climate
    changes,
And the death of the heart
Is required.

Nocturne 3

This business of night must end. It's getting
Unbearable. How long more can it go on
Rehearsing all those old moments of fear
And madness? I would own you, night,
Colonise you with reason or, more
   accurately,
Domesticate you into a comfortable silence
Where I could snore my way through
What they call a great night's sleep.

The ghosts who haunted every occasion
Have come to live and every night
Is replete with a thousand ugly moments
Of hurt and pain and loss. Oh, if I could
Defeat you, Night, by death, I would
Have done it, but heeded the warning
of experience that it was but a long night,
Death itself but an extension of that
Universe of day and suffering. And how do
   we know
Any different?
Scrape the day for love. Hunk the furniture
Of affection into the emptied lot of love,
Save the brain from the ravages of night
From which gentleness was driven,
Made a stranger and the occupant now
The landlady of despair.

The Wall

For Victor Jara

I stand at the wall
And cannot see.
My eyes are blinded by what I know.
My heart breaks,
And the tears flow,
For you, Victor Jara.

Through you flowed
The blood of the people.
Their heart beat was not far
From your wide smile.

Can there be happiness again in my heart
When I know that the poet is dead?
But the voice of the people
Stirs the dark.

The sun shines and blinds
And furrows the brown earth
As it wore all our mothers' faces,
Worn and furrowed.
The smile will break again
On the face of Chile.
For, as Pablo wrote,
The voice of the people
Cannot be silenced.

The rivers will always run.
The rivers are not their rivers.
The sun will shine again.

The sun is not their sun.
The earth will moisten again.
The earth is not their earth.
And the hearts of the people
Will always beat.

Already the murmur is growing.
The clouds are gathering
For the Pitucos*
And, in the poblaciones,
They sing you songs.
Victor Jara, you are not dead.

* Chilean term for "yuppies" or "nouveau riche"

50

The Student Who Wanted To Do An M.A. On God

I'd like to do a thesis on God, she said,
The bright student,
Looking for supervision.
There's a good literature on it,
She said,
Anticipating my obvious first question.

I've been really interested in God,
She said,
Since I was a child.
At home we talked about it all the time.
It seems such an interesting topic
For research.
I know he's written hardly anything
But it's the author himself
That interests me.
She gathered speed.

I was thinking of concentrating on the fact
That he was a woman,
Like Shakespeare
Or even a collective.
I'd really like to get stuck into that.

I talked to a friend in Trinity College
Who said it was really a job
For a Ph.D.
But I'd like you to direct me
In a thesis for an M.A.
On God.
If you don't mind me saying it,

I've often heard you saying it
'Oh, God!',
So I knew you were interested in the area.

We'd have to have an empirical aspect,
I interjected wildly.
To keep the extern happy.
You know what I mean.
There has to be some concrete aspect
To it all.
Extern examiners like that.
It could be the difference
Between an Honours and a Pass.

I've thought of that,
She said.
I was thinking of starting
With prayers for rain.
It should be easy,
With raw data from the Met. Office,
To see if he, she, they,
Make it rain
In dry Augusts,
After prayers for rain in churches.

I was thinking of eliminating deserts,
To keep the topic tight, you see,
And it seemed so logical
To follow that
With a sample survey
Of prayers for fine weather in churches
For the hay in a wet July.

And I could start writing a review of the
    literature
On miracles,
Dead raising,
Lame walking,
Blind seeing,
Rich giving all the loot away,
Poor rejoicing with their poverty.
There seems to be such a wealth of material
When I get stuck in.

She was a bright student.
I told her she would go far
And that if her M.A. thesis turned out right
She could go on to the Holy Ghost
For her Ph.D.
When you're in full steam,
I told her,
Let nothing stop you
And do keep your eye
On the possibility of publication.
Who knows,
We could do something together
On the Holy Trinity.
That's where the real action is.

But for now,
Get stuck into God
And meet me every First Friday
To let me know how it's all going
With the M.A.
On God.

Thank you, she said
And, as she left,
She turned
And with a blush said,
You don't know how much this means to
    me.
I almost said it from habit;
'Thank God'
We got sorted out on God
For my thesis.

The Inter

for Alice Mary

Watching you preparing for the Inter,
My daughter,
I see in the chaos of your room
A bird
Scratching its nest into shape
And, through your door,
As between branches broken
With violence,
Come my words
That startle.

What value
My distraction
From your task?
Yours was the work of shaping,
Making your own order
In the chaos of others' demands.

Oh, I would that I had come
With a whisper,
Edged one twig towards where you saw it.
But I am burdened with
A catalogue
Of prefabricated designs,
Ugly, efficient and guaranteed
To do the job.

When I come again
I will bring silence,
But know,

Even in its noise,
It was love that informed
My bad choice.

Move your twigs
Into the pattern that suits
Your moment
And, not from a distance
I hope
I will look and wonder
At whatever shape
Upon which my love
Rests.

Bank Manager Faints at the Mayor's Ball

The Mayor was dancing with her golden
  chain
Not dangling
But nestling on her ample bosom,
When she turned to the Bank Manager and
  said,
Come on outa that and give us a dance.

He was a frightened man
But knew his duty.
We'll make it a slow one, she said
And he trembled.

Three brandies later,
For the benefit of Bank and a safe Branch,
His call came.

Hold me tight, she said.
I love a tight squeeze for the waltz
And I've no time
For this hi-falutin stuff.

The First Citizen and the Bank
Danced cheek to cheek.
Every usurious fibre was tested
As she breathed on his bald head.
He joked occasionally as she laughed
And missed a step.

Oh, if I had you in my time
On the kitchen floor, she said,

I'd give you a one-two-three
You'd never forget.

The perspiration beaded his brow.
His legs turned to jelly.
His eyes blurred as he sank to the floor.
Dear Jesus, he's fainted, the First Lady said.
What lack of respect for the dignity of my
  office.
But then, I've never trusted the Banks.

They picked him up and said he needed air,
But, taking her handbag and walking away,
She coldly looked at them all,
And simply said,
With all the dignity of the office,

It's a poor thing at the Mayor's Ball
When the Chain can't waltz with safety
With those who for our account
Bought the little box we carry it in.
It isn't air he needs
But a box.

Blowing her nose, she laughed
And the Band played on
At the Mayor's Ball.

Corrib Love

What shall we say then my love
In times to come
When our eyes meet
Shall we dare even remember
A day once on Corrib
When the sun shone
And we took a boat and rowed
And I asked you a question
Shall we make love.

And you, who knows
Perhaps half deliberately
Said no
That day when our flesh was young
And the sun shone
On Corrib
And we had taken a boat.

And now this time
No question allowed
Old flesh condemned to crawl over old flesh
Answer prescribed
Shall we dare even remember
That day on Corrib once
When the sun shone
And I asked you a question
Or shall we after all remember
We saved our souls.

Against All Certainty

There is something so easy about certainty.
In front of the shrine of Saint Jude
The little white haired lady looks anxious.
In the main aisle the middle aged man
In a grey suit and a beautiful, fresh, pink
   face,
Looks certain.

It is, I suppose, something like
The difference between
Saving certificates
And a Lotto ticket.

But, I want her to win with Saint Jude,
At least share the jackpot
And I wouldn't collapse if he
Lost some of his certificates.

Or, is it I envy his certainty?
Recalling times
Leaving the intimate smell
Of the confessional,
I bent my head with that great relief
That forgiveness was certain.
And the sun shone with a blinding energy
In my eyes when I came out.
And the gravel sang to me
Outside the Church
Under my foot.
Days of certainty.
And if it was not for the fact

That God did not call
People like us,
I might have loved to be
Imparting certainty
In a sweaty box
For life.

The scruple is the maggot in the heart of
   certainty.
It is it that breaks the core
With its question.
Are you sure you can be certain
Of anything
For which you should be forgiven?

A man came home from England
And, robbed on the boat
Between Holyhead and the city
He never knew as capital,
Felt he had been judged
For only an occasional Mass
In England,
Punished to return
With a dirty shirt
And an empty pocket.

All us children heard him scream.
Or was it a cry,
For only the Banshee cried
In our village.
And he tore at the roots of the furze

Saying he'd find the gold
That all the old ones missed.
And when they found him,
His face was scraped
As he rubbed his soil-filled nails
Around his wild eyes.

He was never the same.
We children were told
Not to ask questions.
And he never again was able
To go home alone
From games of forty-five.

But, passing up the hill
Where on the old road
The bushes threatened to make a canopy,
One's eyes could not avoid
The shrine stone with its edge of moss
Upon which he knelt
And prayed for forgiveness.

Was it not a holy stone
And if the shift of guilty gravel
Was not in doubt,
Should one not kneel
Not only for him
But for oneself?

The soil under his nails,
And yours,
Was poison.
To clean one's nails in church

Was sacrilege
That could never be told
In a wooden box
Of sweat and a small curtain.
There could never be certainty again.

And if one looks
And hopes the white-haired lady
Wins the jackpot with a little help
From Saint Jude
And if one gazes at the pink face
Of the man more certain,
Is it not a glance in a terrible mirror
Where those more certain
Can smile for ever?

And then if tears are now allowed
The grown person
That was the child,
Is it not better
To be uncertain,
To have the scruple
And throw away the apple
That was certainty?

For now you see them both
That cannot see each other,
Who kneel
And the pain of the heart is real,
And where there was gravel
There is the uncertainty
Of love
That needs the polish

Of a restless wonder,
That gives those glimmers,
Even, on occasions,
That confirms
We make our own uncertain magic.

Between

Timorously hung
Between
Marxism and Post Modernism
Between
Depression and Despair
Between Violetta Chamorro and Daniel
Between
Life and Death
Waiting
For the strength
To say
I'll go on
I try to remember
Certainty
And conclude
It's better
Between

The Death Of The Red Cow

On horse-fly days she occasionally ran
But usually she ambled,
As she led home cows not as experienced
And skittish heifers too.

It was to her a child could be allocated
Where the swish of a dirty tail
Was the only danger.

Measuring her yield
Against the rivets sinking under the foam
In the galvanized bucket,
A child's heart filled with love
As one's forehead pressed her udder
From which, even at five,
You knew how to remove sciartáns*.

Loyalest of providers you loved her
And when the voices woke you at night,
You knew at once
That it was from her stall,
In what adults would like to call a Barn,
That the commotion came.

They tried the nails on her hips
And buckets of gruel were brought
But, when you came,
The stench around her open mouth
Told you
That the red cow was dying.

The lights of the vet's car
Brought hope
But his words were short,
I'm sorry.

And you broke the news to your city mother
Who only said,
Milk was the one thing
We were never short of.

And on the following morning
The Burkes sent potatoes
But life now would change utterly.

The separators basin no longer needed
To be shone,
The steel discs disassembled
And there would be no contest
As to who could last longest
Turning the wheel.
There would be no more measures
Of pints and quarts of her yield.

When the red cow died
Your time for fields was over
And now there would be
The scattering
And the measure only
Of escape
And your own life.

* A maggot found on udders of cows, and that sucks blood.

When Will My Time Come

When will my time come for scenery
And will it be too late
After all?
Decades ago I was never able
To get excited
About filling the lungs with ozone
On Salthill Prom.

And when the strangers
To whom I gave a lift
Spoke to me of the extraordinary
Light in the Western sky,
I often missed its changes.
And, later, when words were required
To intervene at the opening
Of Art Exhibitions,
It was not the same.

What is this tyranny of head
That stifles; the eyes, the senses all
Play on the strings of the heart.

And, if there is a healing,
It is in the depth of a silence
Whose plumbed depths require
A journey through realms of pain
That must be faced alone. The hero,
Setting out, will meet an ally
At a crucial moment. But the journey
Home is mostly alone.

When my time comes, I will have made
My journey. And through my senses
Will explode the evidence of light
And air and water, fire and earth.

I live for that moment.

Dark Memories

Sitting in a dark room, she'd ask me
Not to turn on the light,
That her tears might not be seen.
We'd know it was like that
For, earlier she might have said,
If I was starting out again,
It's into a convent I'd have gone,
Away from all the trouble.
Or she would have spoken
Of lovely times in the shop, drinking
Tea and eating Marietta biscuits,
Or taking a walk with her little dog,
After playing the piano in the sitting-room
Over the shop, where soldiers came
And bought more biscuits, when life
Was easy in Liscarroll,
A garrison town; before my father
Blew up railway lines and courted his way
Into her affections.

She stood straight then, and, in a long
   leather coat,
After her mother died she packed her case
Left and joined him a full decade after
The Civil War. And she had loved him
In her way. Even when old Binchy placed a
   note
Behind the counter in his shop
In Charleville that when all this
   blackguardism
Was over, there would be no jobs
For Republicans in his firm, or anywhere
   else,
For that matter.

Now bent and leaning towards the fire,
With blackened fingers holding the tongs,
She poked the coals; and we knew,
It best to leave her with her sorrow
For her lost life, the house she'd lost,
The anxious days and nights,
And all that might have been.

We ran outside and brought in turf
And did our lessons and vowed that we
   would listen
To what she said, of cities where always
There were voices for company, and
   churches
Close by, if never cheap.
We would listen to her story
And vow that, for her at least,
We, her children, would escape.

The Age Of Flowers

My child woman daughter
Has been given a gift of flowers.
But she wants to gather balloons.

White and red, gold and blue
They float above her bent head.
Her thin fingers,
As she disentangles their gaiety
From the anchor of a chair,
Move with frenzy.

When my irritation shows
She anticipates the suggestion
That it is past the age of balloons.
That the age of flowers is a new season.

They are for the boys, she says.
Seeking refuge in the collective
That is the child's brief allowance
From the tyranny of a life
Where balloons must not be mixed with
   flowers.

Oh my daughter if you only knew
What pain I give myself
To reflect and think
That I have been part
Of the destruction of a child's wonder.

Carry flowers, balloons, blow whistles,
Laugh and jump
My woman child daughter.
Break every binding string.
Stretch every sense.
Break every restriction
Of those impulses without reflection
That make the random utterances
Of the day-release prisoner
Of repression
That is your father.